Animals EAT the WEIRDEST Things

DIANE SWANSON
ILLUSTRATED BY TERRY SMITH

HENRY HOLT AND COMPANY

NEW YORK

Henry Holt and Company, Inc.
Publishers since 1866
115 West 18th Street
New York, New York 10011

Henry Holt is a registered
trademark of Henry Holt and Company, Inc.

First published in the United States in 1998 by
Henry Holt and Company, Inc.
Originally published in Canada in 1998 by Whitecap Books

Edited by Elaine Jones
Proofread by Elizabeth McLean
Cover design by Peter Cocking
Interior design by Warren Clark

Library of Congress Cataloging-in-Publication Data
Swanson, Diane.
    Animals eat the weirdest things / by Diane Swanson: illustrated by Terry Smith.
        p.   cm.
    Includes index.
    Summary: Describes what different animals ingest and why.
    1. Animals—Food—Juvenile literature.   [1. Animals—Food habits.]
I. Smith, Terry, ill.   II. Title.

QL756.5.S8   1997   591.5'3—dc21   97–41980

ISBN 0-8050-5846-X

First American edition—1998

Printed in Singapore on acid-free paper. ∞

1 2 3 4 5 6 7 8 9 10

MENU

ALL SORTS Buffet

You wouldn't want to eat what some animals eat. Think of beetles chomping cigarettes, squirrels nibbling antlers, foxes eating rotting whales, rabbits downing dung, and gulls gobbling vomit. Sound gross? You bet. But among animals, tastes and needs vary a lot.

Almost anything that comes from a plant or animal is food for some critter. Even the wastes and leftovers from one animal are sources of nutrients for another. All around the world, mammals, birds, insects, and others have adapted to eating some surprising things. But when you think about restaurant food such as bird's nest soup, so have people.

Little black flies that are common throughout the world often lay their eggs in dung. When the larvae hatch, they have both food and shelter, even through winter.

Dinner for this herring gull chick will be warm and easy to eat: a chunk of fish that its parent has partly digested.

Doing What Comes Naturally

Animals naturally choose the food they need, mostly letting instinct be their guide. And that can lead them in some unexpected directions.

Take the hawfinch, for example. It's a pretty European bird that attacks cherries when it's hungry. But it doesn't often eat the fruit. As the ripe cherries fall to the ground, it may toss aside their sweet flesh and grab just the stones.

Although the hawfinch is a small bird, its bill is super-strong, and the muscles that work to snap it shut are powerful. Crushing cherry stones is no problem for the hawfinch. It grinds up plum pits and olive stones just as easily. This rocklike food usually takes several days to digest, but it provides much of the nutrition the hawfinch needs.

Some kinds of animals require just a few different kinds of nutrition. Other animals—like people—need many kinds, including:

- protein for growing and repairing worn-out parts (it contains life-essential nitrogen);
- carbohydrates (in starch and sugar) for energy;
- fats for storing energy;
- vitamins for good health and fitness; and
- minerals, such as calcium and phosphorus, for strong bones.

EATING MORE THAN FOOD

Not everything animals eat is food. You've probably seen birds pecking at fine gravel. They're not having a rock dinner—the gravel helps them grind up tough food in a part of their stomach called the gizzard.

Millions of years ago, dinosaurs did the same thing. Some kinds swallowed small stones. In the process, they polished these stones smooth.

In the small stomach of a young grebe, a water bird, researchers found more than 300 feathers. Not only do adult grebes gulp down feathers, they feed some to their chicks. The chicks also pluck and swallow feathers on their own.

A few animals can digest feathers, but grebes can't. So no one knows for sure why they swallow so many. One idea is that the soft feathers may protect the stomach. Grebes eat a lot of fish with very sharp bones.

Finding enough nutritious food can be hard, especially as there are millions and millions of diners searching. That's why animals have adapted to eating so many different—sometimes odd—kinds of food.

And when it comes to obtaining food, there's no free lunch. All animals must pay for what they eat with the energy they use to find it and the dangers they face while searching. They also must pay with their time: finding food is what many animals spend most of their lives doing. So those that eat dung, wood, bones, and other weird—but plentiful—food pay far less than animals that hunt for prey. Eating weird is actually eating smart.

People Eat the Weirdest Things

Animals are not the only ones with unusual appetites. People eat surprising food, too. Many have licked up coal tar as an ingredient in some kinds of ice cream, and people in the Arctic have feasted on partly digested clams taken from the stomach of the walrus.

Around the world, a number of people eat spiders. One favorite is the blue-legged tarantula, which lives underground. It's rich in protein, minerals, and vitamins. Other people prefer the South American goliath tarantula, the largest spider in the world. Its ball-like body

TARANTULA TASTE TREAT

The goliath tarantula of South America is an excellent source of protein, but it can give a hunter an extremely painful bite. Further, the recipe below is only recommended if prepared by a professional spider chef. DO NOT TRY IT YOURSELF.

1. Take one plump goliath tarantula.
2. Squeeze the insides carefully onto a leaf.
3. If the tarantula is female, squeeze out any eggs, too.
4. Roll the whole mass up in the leaf.
5. Put it over a low-burning fire.
6. Stick the tarantula body beside it to toast.
7. Take the rolled leaf and the body from the fire.
8. Remove the hair and fangs from the body, and peel it.
9. Eat all the white meat and the whole mass in the leaf.
10. Pick your teeth with the fangs.

People in Colombia have roasted the bellies of leafcutter ants and eaten them like popcorn.

is up to 3.5 inches (9 centimetres) across. Put it on a dinner plate and all eight feet hang over the edge.

Perhaps one of the oddest human foods is a nest made of bird saliva. In Asia, little birds called swiftlets ooze a sticky saliva from glands beneath their tongue. Then they apply it in layers to the walls or roofs of caves to build clear, rubbery nests. White-nest swiftlets make nests from pure saliva; black-nest swiftlets work some of their feathers into the nests.

Millions of people eat swiftlet nests as a special treat called bird's nest soup. Cooks add spices and chicken to the soup because the nests have almost no taste. They offer almost no nutrition, either. In China, however, people have eaten them for 1500 years, often to recover from sicknesses.

SIDE-ORDER SPECIALS

- In Java, Indonesia, there's an ant that sometimes feeds from the gland of a native bug. But the ooze from the gland gradually paralyzes the ant. Then the bug eats it.
- When birds are producing eggs, they may eat snail shells—as well as the snail's body—to get extra calcium.
- People have eaten some crazy things to set records. In 1977 in France, Monsieur M. Lotito ate a whole bicycle by shredding the metal and stewing the tires. In 1980, Jay Gwaltney of the United States ate a birch tree 11 feet (3.4 metres) tall by nibbling away at the leaves, branches, and trunk over a period of 89 hours.

Thank heaven animals eat weird things. They use their resources well. They help keep this planet clean. And some of their feeding also cleans other animals.

Strong-swimming birds called phalaropes, for instance, clean the backs of whales by eating bits of animals that cling there. Various kinds of small fish swim into the mouths of big fish to gobble up stale and rotting food. And birds such as plovers pick out whatever is stuck between the teeth of crocodiles.

Sea diving birds, such as puffins, sometimes eat dung from whales.

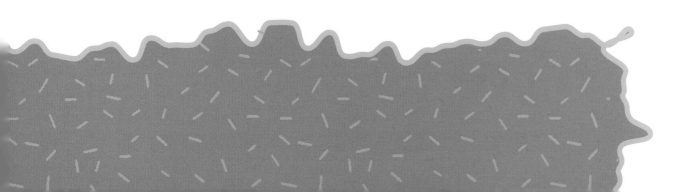

BLOOD, SKIN, and CAST-OFF Parts

People chew fingernails out of habit, not hunger. And it's their own nails they chew, not someone else's. Zookeepers, however, have seen small brown rats gnawing the feet of full-grown elephants. The toenails on these wrinkled giants are rich in oil—food for the rats.

Although rats eat almost anything, they prefer a healthful, well-balanced diet. To get what they need, they turn to many sources. And their ever-sharp, ever-growing front teeth help make the job easy. Rats can slice or gnaw anything from the freshest grass shoots to the toughest toenails. They can even chew their way through metal and concrete to reach the food they want.

Many other kinds of animals use parts and pieces from live creatures as important sources of nutritious food. Some dine by drawing blood. Some feed on skin, including the hair, fur, and feathers that grow from it. And some eat old antlers, shells, and coats that other animals leave behind.

According to zookeepers in London, England, rats nibbling on toenails make elephants "restless."

10

Mmm, Mmm, Blood

During night's darkest hours, vampire bats fly low in search of blood. Common vampire bats of Central and South America sip mostly from sleeping pigs, goats, cows, and horses. Outsized bat ears help them search for hosts. The bats squeal, then listen to the echoes—the sounds that bounce back after striking objects. These echoes make it easier for bats to find their way in the darkness and locate their hosts.

As a vampire bat swoops closer, its super sense of smell helps it zero in on a target. And heat sensors in its fleshy nose pinpoint the best spot to bite. That's usually a warm place, where blood vessels lie close to the surface.

Each night, the common vampire bat needs at least .5 ounce (15 millilitres) of blood—equal to half the bat's own weight.

If the bat finds a hairy food source, such as a horse, it often holds onto the tail or mane. Then its super-sharp teeth make a tiny cut in the horse's neck, shoulder, or rump. As the blood starts to flow, the mouse-sized bat laps it up. Grooves on its tongue and bottom lip direct the blood to the back of its throat. And all the while, chemicals in its saliva keep the blood from clotting.

A bat may feed for up to half an hour. Sometimes another bat or two will join it, lapping at the same cut. Then, with its stomach bulging with blood, the bat heads back to its hollow tree or cave. Unless it is carrying a disease such as rabies, the bat leaves its host unharmed and, usually, still asleep.

If the vampire bat fails to feed for two or three nights in a row, it could die. That's why it's so important for bats to have buddies. Living in colonies—usually of about 100—female bats form bonds with other female bats. If one of them has had a poor night hunting, she licks her buddy to ask her to share some blood. First, she licks under the wing, then on the lips. If the buddy has fed well that night, she brings up some of her blood meal. Mouth to mouth, she passes it to the hungry bat, giving her a chance to live longer. The favor is returned another night if the buddy comes home hungry.

Blood is rich in protein, so many animals besides bats feed on it. A freshwater leech, which is a kind of worm, can take in a meal of blood that weighs 10 times more than the leech itself. For its size—up to 4.5 inches (12 centimetres) long—it eats one of the biggest meals of any animal in the world.

But the leech doesn't feed often; it has pouches inside its body that store blood for months. When it needs food, it swims toward a moving animal, such as a fish, frog, or turtle. The leech is attracted by the ripples that the animal creates as it moves in the water. Then the leech uses a sucker near its tail to crawl over its host, searching for a good area to bite. Many leeches bite by sawing with three curved jaws—each edged like a bread knife—within a sucker around the mouth.

The leech's saliva helps keep the blood flowing while the worm sucks. Once full, the leech is so bloated it can hardly move. So it heads for deeper water and rests among rocks and logs.

Anyone bitten by mosquitoes, bedbugs, or sand flies knows that plenty of insects eat blood, too. Sucking lice—small, wingless insects—often dine on blood, starting with a fresh bite each time. A louse uses three pointed tubes to pierce the skin and suck up some blood. Then it draws the tubes back into its head until the next time it feeds.

Different kinds of sucking lice feed on different kinds of animals. With sharp claws, they cling to the hair or fur of their hosts. Staying very close to a food source is important for lice because they can't survive for long on their own.

One of the most famous blood-sucking insects—found throughout the world—is the tiny flea.

Some moths in Asia suck up blood AND feed on eye-moistening liquid. A scientist spotted a dozen all drinking from an eye of a wild cow.

Blood and Evil

The idea of animals drinking blood from living creatures doesn't appeal to many people, so it's not surprising to find stories that link these animals to evil.

From Europe came tales of vampires who drank human blood at night. The vampires were said to be wicked spirits who lived in the bodies of dead people and sometimes appeared as bats. When they attacked, their victims had frightening nightmares, and some became vampires themselves.

From England came the story that blood-sucking fleas held the souls of evil people. Within these small bodies, the souls couldn't do much damage. But if the bodies had been the size of horses, the story said, they would have killed off much of the country.

Using feelers that sense heat, breathing, and movement, it has little trouble finding its victims.

The flea has no wings, so it moves onto another animal by jumping. Then it uses hooked bristles on its legs to cling to fur or feathers. If necessary, the flea can leap hundreds of times without getting tired. Once on its target, it slips easily between hairs. Then it uses a spearlike mouthpart to pierce the skin and a strawlike part to draw out blood. Its tough coat protects it from any biting and scratching its victims do.

After fleas lay eggs, their young, called larvae, often feed on the dried blood of a flea-bitten animal. From young to old, the lives of some kinds of fleas are in tune with the lives of their hosts. Take rabbit fleas, for example. Their breeding is triggered by the breeding of the rabbits they feed on. That way, the flea larvae hatch when the young rabbits are born—a new blood source for a new generation of fleas.

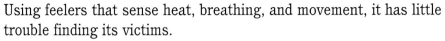

To reach its target, the blood-sucking flea can leap a distance 150 times its length, sometimes turning cartwheels as it goes. That's like a person leaping to the top of the Eiffel Tower in France.

A flea can live for months without feeding, but it's quick to find a meal when it needs one.

Skin-ny Suppers

For some kinds of animals, shed—or molted—skin is a great source of nutrition. Salamanders, for one, feed on animals such as insects, snails, slugs, and worms, but some kinds also eat their own molted skin.

Cousins to frogs and toads, the salamanders—including newts—live both in water and on damp land. They take in water through their soft skin. Many kinds also take in air this way. Salamanders frequently shed their thin, outer layers of skin and replace them with fresh ones. They also shed skin as they grow, struggling to work their way out of it.

For some salamanders, the skin peels off in pieces. For others, it comes off whole. The shed skin is see-through and complete, down to each individual toe. Floating in water, a whole suit of skin looks like a salamander ghost. But if the salamander is going to eat the skin, it doesn't wait long. It swallows the skin, often by taking large amounts into its mouth at a time.

Life among the fur of moles, voles, and shrews is a healthy one for a tiny, blind European beetle. It feasts on dandruff.

In its pond, this rough-skinned newt stuffs itself with its own molted skin.

North America's pronghorn antelopes sometimes eat the layer of skin and special hair that covers their own horns each year. After the breeding season, both male and female antelopes shed their horn coverings, then munch them up. Later, new covers form and harden to protect the horns' permanent core. Antelopes are the only animals in the world that shed and regrow their horn covers.

Several kinds of insects also feed on skin and the protein-rich feathers or fur growing from it. Insects called chewing lice, for example, are so tiny and flat they can easily graze on the bodies of bigger animals. Using strong mouthparts, the lice nibble the feathers and the scaly foot skin of birds such as pigeons, peacocks, and ducks. They also eat the hair of goats, horses, and cows. Lice lay their eggs on their hosts so their young will be surrounded by food when they hatch.

But can you imagine living on dandruff? That's dinner for the eight-legged house-dust mite. A cousin of the spider, it lives in large numbers in house dust everywhere, but it's seldom seen. The mite is only about .01 inch (.025 centimetre) wide.

Of all the bits and pieces that make up house dust, dandruff is the mite's favorite food. But before it eats, it waits for a fungus to attack the dandruff and reduce the amount of fat in it. Fatty foods don't agree with house-dust mites.

As 40-foot (12-metre) gray whales plow the Pacific Ocean, 1-inch (2.5-centimetre) whale lice ride along. Related to crabs, they have several pairs of legs built for clinging to their host. And while they ride, they dine on dead skin and other specks of waste.

THAT'S JUST LOUSY

Many expressions in our language come from the words and feelings we have for animals. We call someone a "louse," for example, if that person is mean and nasty. We don't like having a louse around the house—whether it's an insect or a person.

We also use the word "louse" when we talk about doing something badly. "To louse up" means "to foul up" or "to mess up." That meaning comes from the actions of the insect, which can irritate the skin and damage the fur or feathers of its host.

And "lousy" means infested with lice, but we also use it to describe many things that are totally awful: a lousy idea, a lousy action, or a lousy person.

Yummy Cast-offs

Rabbits, porcupines, chipmunks, squirrels, and mice are a few of the animals that munch on antlers shed by deer. Except for caribou, only the male deer—including moose and elk—form these bony growths on their heads. They are tools that males use mainly in battles for mates.

Most antlers grow best during the summer, when deer find plenty of nutritious food to eat. It takes a lot of calcium and other minerals to grow large, sturdy antlers. When they first form, they are soft. Toward fall, calcium stiffens them and they stop growing. After the breeding season, the males shed their antlers, but they start forming new sets in spring.

The moose produces the biggest antlers of any member of the deer family. They can weigh more than 45 pounds (20 kilograms)—a generous meal for porcupines, squirrels, and other animals.

Soon after the shed antlers hit the ground, animals attack them. Porcupines, for one, have sharp teeth built for gnawing. They can make antlers disappear surprisingly fast. And that's a good thing. The porcupines gain the calcium, phosphorus, protein, and fat in the antlers and clear the land in the process. Imagine the thickets of antlers that would otherwise cover the ground.

Some animals haul off chunks of antlers and store them for eating later. Red squirrels, for instance, stuff these chunks into holes in trees, hide them under rocks, or bury them among cones piled beneath the trees where they feed.

Another rich and crunchy source of calcium is eggshell. You may toss it away when you crack open an egg, but some animals, including a few that lay the eggs, snack on shell after the young have hatched. In the barren northern Arctic, for example, the tiny nestlings of birds called Lapland longspurs depend on the calcium in eggshell to help them grow strong bones. And mother owls sometimes eat up shell after their owlets hatch. It's one way of removing clues that hungry predators might use to find a nest.

Creatures that live in very deep water in the world's oceans have little choice when it comes to food. Their world is so dark that no plants grow. These deep-sea animals, including some kinds of fish, sea stars (also called starfish), and worms, depend on food that drifts down from the surface. And a big part of that food is made up of thin, molted coats from shrimplike animals called krill.

In very cold, snowy winters, magpies and crows may pluck wool from sheep. They can't digest the protein it is made of, but the grease in the wool is a much-needed source of fat.

CHAMPION CHOMPERS

When you think how hard people struggle to bite through a thick carrot, it's amazing that small animals can gnaw moose antlers. What makes that possible is their very special teeth.

The front teeth of rodents, such as porcupines, squirrels, chipmunks, and mice, are super-sharp and super-strong. Layers of hard enamel coat the front of these teeth, but not the back. So when a rodent gnaws on things, it wears away the back of its teeth much faster than the front.

The result? Chisel-shaped teeth that get sharper—not duller—with use. What's more, these teeth never wear out because they never stop growing.

Rabbits are champion chompers, too. Their teeth are so much like rodents' teeth that people used to think rabbits were rodents. But rabbits have two extra teeth right behind their top front pair. Now that's a mouth made for chomping.

As these little plant-eaters grow, they molt their coats again and again. One kind of krill in the Pacific Ocean molts every five days. Unless the molted coats are snapped up along the way, they sink, reaching the deep ocean floor several days later.

In the Antarctic Ocean, krill swarm in huge masses the area of a few football fields and more than 16 feet (5 metres) thick. The krill take only a second to molt and, if threatened, actually leap right out of their coats.

The material that sinks through layers of ocean water soon gathers in the muck on the sea floor. Many deep-sea animals feed by sucking in the muck. Then they digest any useful bits and get rid of the rest. One deep-sea fish called a rattail sucks up mouthfuls of muck from the ocean floor. Its mouth, which is on the bottom of its huge head, is well placed to feed this way. The fish seems to use parts of its gills—called gill rakers— to filter the usable food.

Blood, skin, and other parts from live animals seem to make odd—even disgusting—meals. But the animals that eat these meals are making excellent use of nature. Some are recycling cast-off parts, such as antlers, that would otherwise be wasted and create litter. And think of the many creatures that can feed from just one animal when the meals are food such as blood or feathers.

MMMarvelous Meals

- Small insects called kissing bugs can eat more than 12 times their weight in a meal of blood.

- The eggshell that some animals nibble comes in thick and thin packages. Shell can weigh as little as 5 percent or as much as 15 percent of the weight of the whole egg.

- Some leeches feed on people, but they have helped people, too. Doctors have used leech saliva to prevent blood from clotting and tumors from spreading.

ROTTING
Flesh and Bones

High in the mountains of New Zealand lives the kea, a strong, spunky parrot that hangs around camps and ski resorts. The kea thrives among people. It slides down hut roofs just for fun. It adds table scraps to its meals of insects and plants. And when it finds dead bodies among the sheep herds New Zealanders raise, it dines on flesh. Landing on a dead sheep, the kea uses its beak like a meat hook. Its beak is longer and less curved than those of most other kinds of parrots, but it's just as strong and sharp.

Keas and other animals that feed on dead and decaying bodies are called scavengers. They move in after animals have already lost their lives to predators, diseases, or accidents. On land and underwater, scavengers include a wide range of big and little birds, mammals, insects, and others.

Some are part-time scavengers that add rotting flesh, called carrion, to their diets. Others are full-time scavengers, eating only carrion and bones. Amazingly, all scavengers get nutrition from carrion without getting sick.

Nature's garbage collectors, the gulls, often follow fishing boats and grab fish innards that are tossed overboard.

With a beak strong enough to drag off a hammer, the kea has no trouble digging into a dead sheep.

Bird Feed

Carrion makes excellent bird feed for many feathered animals, including the bald eagle. With powerful feet, sharp claws, and a strong beak, the eagle is a mighty hunter. It snatches live fish from the water and rabbits from the ground. But it also feeds on dead animals when they're handy. Each fall, when many North American rivers brim with the bodies of salmon that have died after depositing their eggs, bald eagles just help themselves to an easy meal.

The digestive system of the turkey vulture is tough. Without even feeling queasy, this bird can swallow flesh so rotten it oozes poison— enough to kill at least a hundred people.

Hoping for a lunch of leftovers after a kill, some kinds of birds watch predators. Ravens, for instance, watch bears or wolves on the hunt. If these predators attack a large animal, such as an elk, the ravens eat well after the killers have feasted. The birds also listen for the sounds of a hunt. The howling of wolves after a successful kill draws ravens at once.

Sometimes it's easier to find prey than it is to find predators. If a raven discovers a herd of caribou, for instance, it may travel a long distance with them. It hangs around the herd until a wolf pack arrives to make a kill.

But the greatest scavengers are vultures—big birds with long, broad wings and, mostly, naked heads and necks. Worldwide, there are several different species, and when any of them finds carrion, it disappears fast. No matter how much they eat or how rotten the food is, vultures don't seem to get sick.

Soaring through the skies of North and South America, the turkey vulture searches out its food. Some days it flies long distances, riding high on rising bubbles of warm air. It has a sense of smell, but the vulture depends more on its keen sight to find carrion. It also scans the skies for other vultures that are looking for food. If a vulture spots something and lands, others follow. That's why dozens of vultures may suddenly appear from different directions and gather around one body, or carcass.

Turkey vultures, like this one, darkened North American skies when hunters of the 1800s killed buffaloes by the millions.

If turkey vultures find a fresh kill, they must wait for decay or other scavengers to open it up. Their weak beaks can't tear into bodies like the beaks of eagles can. But once a carcass has been opened, a vulture can plunge its head right in. Being bald is helpful at times like this; bits of rotting flesh can't cling to the vulture's head. Instead, the turkey vulture can do what it does best—scrape the bones clean with its rough, filelike tongue.

Bone Breaker Bird

The lammergeier—or bearded vulture—of Europe, Asia, and Africa has earned another name: bone breaker bird. This big vulture is not fast enough to compete well for carrion, so it eats the bones other scavengers leave behind. It can swallow bones as big as 10 inches (25 centimetres) long and 4 inches (10 centimetres) thick. But it breaks larger bones into meal-sized chunks by dropping them from high in the air.

Being a bone eater means that the bone breaker bird doesn't need to be bald. And it isn't. Unlike vultures that are always poking their heads into sticky carcasses, the bone breaker bird can afford to have a handsome head of feathers.

25

Insect Feed

All over the world, mini-scavengers—insects—nibble and scrape carrion and bones. Some scoop up the bodies of other insects as part of their diet. Others feed on nothing but dead flesh from many different kinds of animals.

One of the most fascinating scavengers in the insect world buries dead bodies as food for its young. The common burying beetle uses the joints in its feelers, or antennae, to sniff out a body, such as a mouse or a bird, that is starting to decay.

The smell attracts many burying beetles. They burrow beneath the body and, bit by bit, push the soil out from under it. As they work, the body gradually sinks, often curling up. The whole job takes 2 to 10 hours. Then one pair of burying beetles chases away the others and covers the body with soil. The pair mates, and the female lays her eggs in a chamber she digs nearby. She may also chew a shallow crater in the body and fill it with some of her digestive juices.

When the eggs hatch, the larvae slowly gather around the crater. Their mother takes food from this crater to feed them, mouth to mouth. The feedings continue at least twice an hour until the larvae can eat the carrion on their own.

When burying beetles dig "graves," they work as fast as they can to keep other animals away from their carrion. But flies often find it first. They lay their eggs on carrion so their own larvae will have food when they hatch. Sometimes burying beetles remove the fly eggs by biting off all the hair on the carrion.

Common burying beetles cover food for their young. If this mouse had died on hard ground, the pair would have worked with others to move it to softer soil for burying.

Many kinds of flies feed on protein in dead animals. Bluebottle flies, for instance, follow their keen sense of smell to find an animal that has just died, even if they must fly a long distance. They lay their eggs in the carrion, and their wormlike larvae soon hatch.

At first, the larvae feed on liquid inside muscles. As they do, their droppings dissolve tissues, exposing the parts of the muscles that the larvae want to chew. The more larvae there are, the more droppings there are, and the easier it is for all of them to eat.

Sometimes fly larvae also feed on decaying tissue in wounds. Long ago, military doctors discovered that wounds with blow fly larvae healed better than wounds without. The larvae oozed a liquid that helped the wounds heal.

Rotten Flesh for Furry Feeders

Menus of many mammals feature carrion as part-time food. Some mammals also chew the bones of dead animals, which are a good source of calcium, phosphorus, and some kinds of protein. That's why female mammals such as rats and squirrels chew bones, especially when they are pregnant.

In North and South America, opossums—mammals the size of very small dogs—feed on fish, birds, lizards, frogs, rabbits, and more. They even eat poisonous snakes without suffering from the poison. Sometimes they kill their prey, but they also eat a lot of carrion.

The opossum usually searches for food at night. Whiskers on its nose and cheeks help it feel its way in the dark. The opossum may travel several miles (many kilometres), sniffing for the scent of food as it walks. It holds its nose close to the ground, but it can easily sniff its way up a tree. The opossum is a great climber, able to grab branches with its tail as well as its paws.

Crawling with Clues

Insects help solve mysteries. After a murder, they are usually the first to reach the victim. That's why detectives check the crime scene for insects, searching the victim's body and clothing, too. They note the kinds of insects, their ages, and the stages of life they are in. The insects are important clues that help pinpoint the time of the murder. They also help detectives decide if the body had been moved and if the victim had been taking drugs.

Using insects to solve crimes is not new. About 700 years ago, a man was trying to solve a murder in a farming region in China. He suspected the murder weapon was a sickle—a sharp, curved blade used to cut grain. The man called together all the farmers in the region and asked them to lay their sickles down. He knew that even tiny specks of blood stuck on the sickles would attract flies. As flies gathered on one of the blades, the man accused its owner of murder. The farmer confessed.

Living at the top of the world, the Arctic fox eats whatever it can, and that includes carrion. In the harshest northlands of Europe, Asia, and North America, this small fox hunts mouselike lemmings, ground squirrels, and birds, but it also eats dead seals and walruses that have washed ashore. And rotting whales make humongous meals!

Using its great sense of smell, the Arctic fox often travels far to find food. Sometimes it searches across ice that blankets parts of the ocean in winter. And it may follow a polar bear on a hunt, then wait quietly to clean up scraps.

The wolverine is digging a hole to store food. Its large, furry feet act like snowshoes, keeping the wolverine from sinking in deep snow.

Sharing some of the world of the Arctic fox is a bearlike creature with a big head, strong jaws, and bone-crushing teeth. The wolverine looks like the fierce killer that it is, but it actually eats more rotting meat than fresh meat. Instead of hunting, it may travel over 19 miles (30 kilometres) in a night, searching for carrion.

With long, sharp claws, the wolverine might rip open a log to steal food stored by a bear. It might drive away a mountain lion to grab its kill. It might track a fur trapper to snatch rotting bait and animals from steel traps.

What it doesn't devour on the spot, the wolverine will stash. Strong enough to drag a carcass three times heavier than itself, it looks for a good area to bury its food. It usually rips the carrion apart and stores each chunk separately. It might dig a deep storage hole or yank a hunk of carrion up a tree and wedge it between the trunk and a rising branch. Then it takes off again, knowing it has a ready-to-eat meal waiting.

One of Africa's best-known scavengers is the hyena, especially the spotted hyena. But it's less of a scavenger than many people think. Just one-quarter of its food is carrion, which the hyena usually eats during the day. At night, it chases and kills prey.

Finding carrion is easier in daylight, when hyenas can watch for vultures. These big birds fly high, scanning the ground for carcasses. The hyenas keep the birds in view, ready to run when the vultures spot food and touch down.

When it moves in on a carcass, the hyena carries off parts that other animals cannot. Its jaws can crush the leg of a rhinoceros, and its teeth are specially built for cutting, tearing, and grinding. A set of back teeth work like strong shears, slicing through even the toughest hide.

When hyenas have a whole carcass to themselves, they eat almost every part. They can reduce a large antelope to a set of horns and teeth. The only thing that their heavy-duty stomachs reject later is hair.

Hyenas usually hide leftovers. They may plop carrion into calm, muddy water just deep enough to keep land scavengers from seeing or smelling it. Within a day, the hyenas usually return to fetch it. They seem to remember generally where they have hidden the carrion, but they have to poke their heads into the water at several places to find it. What they fail to find is their loss, but it may be another scavenger's gain—underwater.

The big, ever-alert ears of the hyena can hear the sounds of chomping from as far away as 2 miles (3 kilometres). Then the hyena takes off, its ears leading the way to its next meal.

The Werehyenas

You've likely heard stories of werewolves—mythical people who turned into wolves, then back into humans. A lot of these stories came from Europe, where many wolves once roamed.

In Africa, there are many hyenas, so it's not surprising to find stories of werehyenas. One tale tells of an army captain who wounded a hyena that was searching a village for food. But when the captain tried to track it through the bush, he found only the hyena's jawbone in a puddle of blood. Villagers later claimed the captain had killed one of their men—a werehyena who had stumbled home before dropping dead. He had been shot in the face and his jaw was missing.

Rotten Flesh Underwater

Every year, about 500 gray whales die along North America's Pacific coast. Some are eaten by predators, but many whale bodies become gigantic lumps of food for scavengers. The carcasses can weigh up to 81,400 pounds (37 000 kilograms) each. Some animals feed on them as they sink. And whatever is left when they hit bottom forms a banquet for sea floor critters.

Sea stars, for example, scrounge carrion of all kinds along most coasts. Creeping over the sea floor, they also prey on live animals, such as clams.

A sea star is mostly a stomach with arms. Its mouth is on its underside, so when the sea star eats, it drapes itself over its dinner. Many kinds of sea stars feed by turning their stomachs inside out and poking them through their mouths. Sea stars that can't stick out their stomachs swallow whole animals such as snails, then they cast out the shells.

But of all the scavengers in the seas, the hagfish is one of the most surprising. It's a fish so simple that it has no scales, no fins, no eyes, no jaws, no bones, and no stomach. It can live on muddy sea floors for months without eating anything at all. But when it's hungry, it snakes its way slowly through the water, sniffing for dead fish. As it gets close, fleshy tentacles around its mouth help it feel for food.

When the hagfish finds a dead fish, it wriggles right inside. It may enter through an opening such as the gill slits, mouth, or anus. Or it may use its tooth-covered tongue to scrape a hole in the side of the body. Once the hagfish has worked its way inside, it puts its tongue to use again. It scrapes out all the soft, fleshy parts of the dead fish. Then it exits the same way it entered, leaving an empty bag of skin and bones behind.

Freshwater Jaws

In many lakes and streams, crocodiles prey on animals as large as the hippopotamus, but they also grab carrion when they can.

River currents may sweep up land animals that die along shore and carry them right to the jaws of the crocodile. And hyenas sometimes hide carrion in muddy water, only to have a lucky crocodile snatch it up.

Occasionally, crocodiles leave the water to search for a rotting meal. Hunters once spotted four of the big reptiles feasting on a dead elephant half a mile (800 metres) from a river.

Eating rotting flesh and bones saves many animals the trouble of killing their own food for at least part of their diet. And it makes good use of animals that have already lost their lives.

What's more, scavengers save a great many lives. By cleaning up decay and removing dangerous germs from soil and water, they create a healthier home for all animals.

ROTTEN FEASTS

- White-backed vultures of Africa depend on big meat-eaters, such as lions, to break bones into bits for their chicks to eat.
- What big-mouthed hyenas can't eat, little moths can! Masses of moth larvae can turn the horns on a wildebeest carcass to powder.
- Even the lynx—a swift, skilled hunter—eats carrion. This wild cat of North America, Europe, and Asia depends on rotting flesh to survive winter.
- It's a mystery how scavenging hagfish escape so many diseases. They produce no antibodies that fight off sickness.

Scraping its way into the body of a dead fish, this Pacific hagfish ties itself into a knot. By pressing the knot against the body, the hagfish can scrape even harder.

OOZE, Vomit, and Dung

You wouldn't expect to see ax handles or boat oars on a menu. But almost any wood that's been held in sweaty hands is great food to porcupines. They are drawn to the salt in people's sweat. Sometimes they also gnaw corners of wooden buildings, such as sheds, that animals have sprayed with salty urine.

North American porcupines often eat wood, especially in winter, when they munch the bark and sapwood of trees. Like other rodents, porcupines have large, sharp front teeth and powerful jaws. And they have evolved a way of getting nutrients from the wood. Laced with sweat or urine, the wood is even better food—a source of the salt that porcupines need.

As strange as it seems, many animals eagerly gobble up things that other animals expel. Some take in sweat, urine, and other materials that ooze out of animals. Some eat vomit. Some eat dung. From tiny insects to birds and mammals, many different creatures get part or all of their meals from things we would never call food.

The droppings of bats contain urine, a source of nitrogen for dung-eating insects.

The porcupine eats sweat-soaked slivers of wood almost as prickly as the barbed quills on its back.

Oodles of Ooze

Like porcupines, mountain goats get salt where they can. Clinging to steep slopes of mountains in North America, the goats don't have many choices. The plants they eat contain little salt. Heavy mountain rain and snow wash much of it out of the soil that the plants grow in. So mountain goats get some of the salt and the nitrogen they need by lapping up puddles of urine or nibbling urine-soaked ground.

Many insects, including some butterflies and moths, feed on urine and sweat. Others live inside the noses and sinuses of animals. In these cozy spots, meals of blood and mucus supply all the nutrients they need. Sheep bot flies, for instance, leave their yellowish larvae on the noses of sheep and goats in North America. The larvae make their way to their hosts' sinuses where they live and feed, often staying until they mature.

In return for providing all this food and shelter, the host gets a headache and a runny nose. As it snorts and sneezes, the grown sheep bot flies crawl out through the nostrils.

All around the world, many kinds of ants thrive on honeydew. It's a sweet, sticky liquid that plant-feeding insects, such as aphids, excrete. A tiny aphid produces a lot of honeydew; some kinds produce up to 48 drops a day. Ants just lick it up from leaves when it falls. Or they use their antennae to stroke the aphid, encouraging it to excrete.

Getting plenty of honeydew is easy for ants. Aphids tend to group together, and they don't move around much. That saves ants the time and effort of chasing after their food. Some kinds of ants make getting honeydew even easier, by herding aphids into their ant nest at night. Some ants keep aphids through the winter.

The aphids gain from all this attention. The ants protect them from danger by driving away aphid-eating insects, such as ladybugs. If necessary, the ants even carry aphids to a safer place. In fact, with ants around, aphids seem to grow faster and produce more aphids.

But in an odd twist, there's a mosquito in Africa that steals aphid honeydew

Sweat bees were named for their habit of lapping sweat. Their tongues are short and pointed for the purpose.

from ants. It flies close to tree trunks where the ants are feeding from aphids. Shaking its wings, a mosquito drops down in front of an ant and may use its antennae to stroke it. When the ant opens its mouth, the mosquito pokes in a long, strawlike mouthpart and sucks out the honeydew.

Some bees build honeycombs from wax made by glands inside their bodies. The wax oozes out, forming flakes that the bees chew, then use for building. But it's also food for small birds called honeyguides. In fact, the black-throated honeyguide of Africa can live for a month on nothing but beeswax. Special bacteria in its intestines help it digest the wax.

The honeyguide is good at finding bee nests, but it needs help breaking into them. So it chatters excitedly to attract a badgerlike animal called a ratel. Swooping and prattling, the honeyguide leads the way to the nest. The ratel rips it open with its long, sharp claws; its thick skin protects it from bee stings. Then both animals dine: the honeyguide on the wax and some bee larvae; the ratel on the larvae and some honey.

As bees make wax, spiders make silk. When the silk comes out of little organs at the spider's back end, it hardens into elastic threads. Orb web spiders use some of their silk to make orb— or circle—webs. Some webs are tiny; others are huge. The golden orb weaver of Central and South America makes gold-colored webs that are almost as tall as a doorway.

"Ke, ke, ke, ke, ke, ke, ke, ke, ke," calls a black-throated honeyguide to a ratel. That means, "I've found a honeycomb. Come and get it." Some honeyguides also lead people to honey.

Webs are not only useful for trapping prey, such as insects, they also make wholesome food. The silk is made of protein. When spiders remove whole webs or damaged strands, they eat up the old silk. Digestive ooze from the spider's mouth turns the silk back into liquid. The spider gets extra nutrients from the bits of plants and animals stuck to the web. Many orb web spiders replace a web every 24 hours, eating the old one while spinning the new.

Valuable Vomit

People would much rather dine on soup or stew than on vomit. But to many animals, vomit is a handy, nutritious food. Not only is it ready to eat, it's already partly digested. That's especially useful for young animals.

Mammals, such as wolves, first feed their young ones milk. But when wolf pups are ready for something more, vomit makes a soft, warm food. It's also easy to haul around. If a wolf pack is hunting food far from the den, the wolves can carry it home in their stomachs.

At the den, the pups lick an adult's face and paw its mouth. That's how they say, "Feed me." The adult wolf responds with a big heave—and dinner is served.

Unlike many birds, turkey vultures in North and South America don't have feet or beaks that can carry food. They have to airlift it home in their stomachs. When they return to young vultures in hollow logs or ground nests, they bring up the rotting meat they have eaten. The foul vomit not only feeds the young, it smells up the nest. That helps keep the family safe by repelling skunks and raccoons.

American white pelicans also vomit for their chicks. The adult eats a lot of fish, scooping them up in the stretchy pouch beneath its bill. Then the pelican returns to the nest and shakes its chicks roughly by the head. That's how it encourages them to eat. Then the parent bird drips a thin fish "soup" into the bill of the chicks.

When they are about 10 days old and able to sit up, the chicks poke their bills into their parent's pouch to eat. The bigger the chicks get, the more roughly they feed. They may even chase their parents, pecking their bills for food.

Some animals steal vomit from others. When an Antarctic penguin is feeding vomit to its chick, a dovelike sheathbill may throw itself against the penguin's head. As soon as the food plops on the ground, the sheathbill snatches it.

A gull-like seabird, called the great skua, steals food from smaller birds such as gannets. It usually forces its victim down from the sky. A very strong flier, the skua circles above a gannet, then dives at it. Down to the water they go. The skua grabs the gannet's wing tip and flips it into the ocean. If the gannet flies away, the great skua attacks again until its victim vomits.

In rotting wood or underground nests, vomit is important food for helpless ant larvae. Adult ants that act as nurses care for these larvae, carrying them around and feeding them. Dinner is either thin vomit or partly chewed insects.

Vultures not only feed their young vomit, they use it as a weapon. Both adults and young may throw up when threatened.

Time to eat! This American white pelican chick is so excited, it is nearly crawling inside its parent's bill.

As soon as it hatches, a herring gull chick pecks at a red dot on its parent's bill. The parent vomits up half-digested food, picks up a chunk, and gives it to the chick. Then the chick pecks the bill for more.

Some years ago, world-famous scientist Niko Tinbergen went to a herring gull colony to discover what attracts chicks to their parents' bill. He presented newly hatched chicks with several cardboard gull heads. The bills on these heads had dots of red, black, blue, or white. One had no dot at all.

Tinbergen discovered that the red dot on a herring gull's bill was very important in attracting chicks to peck for food.

But sometimes, uninvited guests come to dinner. In fact, they move right in. Some members of a large family called rove beetles lay their eggs in ant nests. When the beetle larvae hatch, they produce a smell that encourages ants to look after them. The young beetles act like ant larvae, begging for vomit by tapping an ant's mouth with their own. The ants even carry the mimics away from the nest if danger threatens. Meanwhile, the rove beetles take extra advantage of living in the nest by eating ant eggs and larvae.

Using its antennae and legs, a rove beetle taps an ant to request—and receive—some vomit for dinner.

Dung Dinners

Eating dung doesn't sound like a great idea. But for many animals, it's the best way to dine. There's a lot of dung around. And it provides ready-to-use nutrients: crushed vegetable cells with many vitamins and predigested proteins.

In the deep, dark sea, dung is one of few foods that appear daily. Some comes from deep-sea creatures, but much drifts down from animals that live near the surface. Shrimplike animals called copepods are important dung suppliers. So many live in the oceans that people call them "insects of the sea."

Copepods stuff themselves with tiny plant cells. And every day they empty their intestines up to six times, providing food for many animals, such as sea stars.

Some mammals, including rabbits, eat their own dung. They chew up plants, but don't completely digest them. Then the "waste" passes out as soft pellets, which the rabbits eat as soon as they appear. That's how they get more vitamins from their food.

In western North America, the mountain beaver—no relation to the common beaver—does a similar thing. It feeds on plants, which it digests as well as it can. Then it uses its teeth to grab dung as it comes out. Like the rabbit, the mountain beaver eats the pellets to get more nutrients.

Close to its underground burrow, a mountain beaver gets ready to receive some fresh dung.

But the most fascinating dung eaters anywhere are dung beetles. For more than 75 million years, they have been sniffing out dung—first from dinosaurs, later from mammals. The smell draws the beetles fast. On a vast African plain, for instance, it takes no more than 10 minutes for hundreds of beetles to pick up the scent of fresh dung and move in.

Around the world, there are thousands of kinds of dung beetles. Some pull bits of dung into feeding burrows—tunnels they dig in the ground. Most need fresh, moist dung to eat. But some beetles store dry dung in tunnels, where it absorbs moisture during heavy rains.

Some dung beetles not only eat dung but carry it into tunnels to use as nesting material for their eggs and as food for their young. A female beetle might stash some in an opening at the end of one tunnel, rolling it into a ball. Then she might lay an egg in the dung and cover it with a light blanket of dung. She may set up more masses to receive more eggs.

In the driest parts of Australia, some dung beetles ride around on wallabies—members of the kangaroo family. The beetles gather on the rear end of these jumpers so they can leap to the ground when fresh dung falls. Being right on the spot when the dung first appears is good for the beetles. They can bury it before it dries and hardens in the intense heat.

MAKING MUMMIES

Ancient Egyptians had special respect for a dung beetle called a scarab. They thought its head looked like the rising sun. When it rolled a ball of dung, they thought of their god Khepri rolling the sun across the sky. They believed the insect was sacred, so some Egyptians wore strings of dried scarab beetles. Some people put dried beetles in tombs with the dead.

The Egyptians also valued cows and the cow dung that scarabs rolled into balls. When they saw new beetles coming out of these dung balls, they thought the scarabs were coming back to life after being buried.

Today some researchers think that scarabs may have given Egyptians the idea of making mummies—preserving bodies so people might live again.

Other beetles may shape some dung into a ball and roll it a long way to make it more compact. Two beetles may work together on this project—one pushing and one pulling the ball. They mostly use their back legs, often standing with their heads down on their front legs.

Then the dung beetles bury the ball by digging out the soil beneath it. A female beetle lays an egg in it. When the larva hatches, the ball provides both food and shelter.

Crows snatch up chunks of dung dropped by many animals, sometimes storing it under soil or grass for eating later.

Imagine a world piled high with dung and other wastes from animals. That's not a pretty sight. So it's a good thing for everyone that there are dung eaters—and animals that feed on vomit and ooze, too. They help convert all that waste into useful matter for themselves and for the world. In parts of Texas, for example, dung beetles remove about 80 percent of the dung from huge cattle ranches. Then they quickly return this manure to the soil, where it helps plants grow.

Appealing Appetizers

- In dry parts of the world, thick masses of dung beetles follow herds of sheep and camels to collect dung.

- As their name suggests, eye gnats feed on eye fluids. But these tiny members of the fly family also eat pus and mucus.

- Some kinds of wasps and stingless bees tickle treehoppers—sap-sucking insects—to encourage them to excrete honeydew.

- Not fussy feeders, face flies, which look a lot like house flies, feast on anything that oozes from a cow: tears, mucus, milk, saliva, blood, urine, and vomit. A hundred flies may gather on the eyes, ears, nose, and lips of one cow.

MOM, DAD, and the K.i.d.s.

When a grown Dungeness crab rips apart a young Dungeness crab, it's just being crabby—doing what crabs do. Up and down North America's west coast, this crab captures and eats prey such as clams and small fish. But it also eats young crabs, even if they're its own offspring.

Holding them in strong pincers, the crab easily tears young crabs into chunks. Then it uses small feeding parts to move the chunks to its crusty jaws for crushing.

Animals that eat others of their own kind are called cannibals. Some kill their prey. Others feed on animals that have already died. Either way, the cannibals gain food that is well suited to them. The proteins and other nutrients in it match the ones in their own bodies.

From insects to mammals, about 140 kinds of animals normally feed as cannibals. Many others eat their own kind under special conditions. For example, goldfish may eat each other when they're too crowded. And small water insects called backswimmers turn to cannibalism when there's not enough food.

If a Dungeness crab could think, it would rather be old than young. The adults often eat young crabs.

Scrumptious Kids

Among cannibals, it is easier, and more common, for adults to eat the young than it is to eat other adults. For instance, female spiders may gobble up tiny spiders, even ones that are close relatives. And storks—well known in stories for delivering babies—sometimes attack and eat their own. But that's usually when they have been upset. Predators, for example, may have come too close to their nests.

If she's feeling crowded and short of food, a mother mouse may kill a few of her young and share the meat with her remaining babies. The ones that live have a better chance of growing bigger and surviving. But overcrowded mice might attack the young of another family instead. Other rodents, such as ground squirrels and muskrats, might do this, too.

In some families, the kids eat each other. One of the oddest examples is the spadefoot toad family. In dry parts of North America, Europe, and Asia, the larvae—called tadpoles— may hatch in puddles caused by heavy spring rains. They nibble bits of rotting leaves and tiny green algae in the water.

A race against time! Trying to mature before its puddle dries up, this huge spadefoot tadpole eats its sibling.

But some of the tadpoles in the same puddle—and the same family—develop jaws and teeth that are different from their plant-eating brothers and sisters. These tadpoles become meat-eating cannibals that grow much faster and bigger than the others. If the puddle dries up before the plant-eating tadpoles become adults, their cannibal brothers and sisters survive by eating all the others. That's how the spadefoot toad manages to live on.

In some other families, the kids eat each other even before they are born. The European black alpine salamander, for instance, gives birth in the woods to up to four young. That's not a big family, considering the mother often starts with up to 60 fertile eggs. But as the salamanders begin hatching inside her, they gobble up many of the unhatched eggs and eat most of their brothers and sisters.

Mouth-watering Moms

In the whole insect world, there are few mothers as good as earwigs. In fact, most insect mothers just lay their eggs and leave them. But the earwig deposits up to 80 eggs in a narrow crack and stays to protect them. She licks them often to keep them clean and moist. If her den becomes too damp for the eggs, she uses her mouth to move them, one by one.

After the eggs hatch, the earwig mother looks after her young. She lets them curl up under her body and fetches any that stray away. Although she's shorter than a paper clip, she tries to protect her young from lizards and birds. To turn away enemies, she may squirt a foul-smelling liquid from a gland near her back end.

Bad Dad

The ancient Greeks told a story of an evil god called Kronos, who had seized control of the world. He received a warning that one of his children might steal his power and position. So alarmed was Kronos that he swallowed all of his babies as soon as they were born.

His wife, however, decided to trick Kronos. When her son Zeus was born, she wrapped up a stone instead of the baby. She gave the stone to Kronos to swallow, and whisked Zeus to an island to grow up in secret.

When Zeus became a man, he returned home and defeated Kronos. Zeus became the king of the gods. But from Kronos came a new word for the English language: kronism. It means the eating of one's own children.

ACCIDENTAL CANNIBAL

Soft coral polyps don't really mean to eat each other. It just happens. They're tiny, tubelike animals that live in colonies, mostly in warm seas.

Where coral polyps have plenty of light and room, they live in peace, feeding on tiny sea life that floats past. But when they get too crowded, the close contact seems to spark attacks among some kinds. Stronger polyps stick out some of their digestive organs over the weaker polyps, eating the victims where they stand. So what begins as a competition for light and space becomes a feeding frenzy.

As the young get older, the earwig mother may leave them to start a new family. If she stays, she grows weak and dies. Even in death, she continues to help her family: she makes an excellent, nourishing meal for her young before they go their separate ways.

In Australia, there's a spider mother that builds a nest for her young and catches big insects to feed them. These spiders depend on their mom until they can make their own nests and catch their own food.

As they grow bigger, they begin to nibble their mother's legs. They nibble and nibble until she can barely walk. When she can't move at all, they eat the rest of her. By feeding on their mother, the young spiders not only get a healthful meal, they attack fewer of their brothers and sisters. That helps them survive.

As good a mother as the earwig is, she might end up as lunch for her children.

Delicious Dads

Meet the mantids. They live around the world, preying on several different kinds of insects, including other mantids. In fact, some female mantids even kill and eat their mates. For many young mantids, dad has died and disappeared long before they have hatched.

Looking for a mate, a male mantid is often attracted by the smell of a female. He creeps up behind her—slowly and carefully. An hour may pass before he has moved 12 inches (30 centimetres). Then he leaps onto the female and starts the mating process.

The female mantid may turn her head around and bite off his. But that doesn't stop the male from mating. Nerve centers in other parts of his body control some of his movements. In fact, even if the male loses his head *before* he begins mating, these nerve centers guide his legs. He might walk in circles until he bumps into the female, climbs onto her back, and mates.

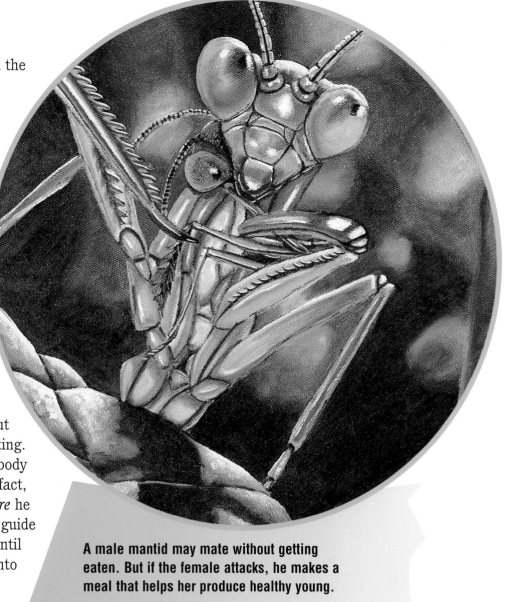

A male mantid may mate without getting eaten. But if the female attacks, he makes a meal that helps her produce healthy young.

PEOPLE AS CANNIBALS

Hundreds of years ago, Europeans formed the word "cannibals" from *Canibales*, a name used for the Carib people, who lived on islands in the Caribbean Sea. The Caribs fought many wars. And they seemed to believe they gained the strength of their enemies by eating them.

People in other parts of the world have also practiced cannibalism. Some believed in religions that called for making—and eating—human sacrifices. Some believed they could gain magical powers through cannibalism. Others simply thought that eating humans was not much different from eating animals. They bought and sold human meat at food markets.

Among spiders that spin circle webs, the females—up to 1000 times heavier than the males—often kill and eat their mates. Males that escape usually die soon after.

One of the most famous spiders to eat the father of her young is the black widow spider. It was named for the female's habit of making herself a widow after mating.

Around the world, especially in warm spots, she builds her web in dark places: inside holes in the ground, beneath rocks, and in corners of basements and garages. Then she tends to stay put, waiting—belly up—to catch her insect prey. She has a set of sacs filled with poison 15 times stronger than rattlesnake poison. When she bites her victims, the poison dissolves their insides.

The smaller male, whose bite is much less poisonous, approaches the female's web carefully. He may bring food for her so she is less interested in eating him. But after they mate, she most likely eats him anyway.

Among many animals, eating their own kind is a normal part of life. For some, it is the only way for their young to survive. Although it seems gruesome to us, cannibalism among animals is just another example of nature finding a way.

FAMILY DINNERS

- Put lobsters in a tank, and they try to feast on each other. Even a two-week-old lobster will attack and eat its brother or sister.

- Insects called lacewings make a "stem" to hold each of their eggs. Then the first lacewing that hatches can't reach the others and eat them.

- Some crows eat crow eggs and chicks, which cuts down the competition for territories, or homes.

- The spotted hyena of Africa feeds on other hyenas now and then. But it doesn't devour hyena meat with its usual zest for food. Instead, it feeds quite slowly.

Boats, Books, and BLANKETS

Look in a vase from the tomb of Egyptian King Tutankhamen, and what do you find? The remains of drugstore and cigarette beetles. More than 3000 years ago, these insects were feeding on baskets and sandals buried with the king.

It's easy to understand how the beetles slipped inside the tomb. They're only .1 inch (.25 centimetre) long. Even today, they slip unnoticed into homes, stores—almost any place they might find food. Sometimes they get into drugstores. Drugstore beetles eat almost any kind of medicine and many other dry products, including makeup, such as face powder.

Drugstore beetles share many food tastes with their close relatives, cigarette beetles. But you might guess that these relatives prefer eating cigarettes and cigars—even the packages they come in. This habit seems especially strange when you realize that the nicotine in cigarettes and cigars has been used for years to kill many insects.

All around the world, cigarette beetles eat people-made products. Even in ancient Egypt, they crept into tombs and nibbled on straw sandals.

Many kinds of animals, especially insects, eat things that people make. They help themselves to much of the food people produce. And beyond that, some eat things, such as tobacco, that humans would never eat. There are those that feed on wooden boats, houses, and furniture. Others chew on paper, including pages in magazines and books, and even book covers and glue. Still others eat all sorts of material used to make blankets, clothing, and carpets. As strange as this food seems, many animals are able to get some—or all—of the nutrition they need from it.

Wood Is Good!

As food, wood is not high quality, and it's not easy to digest. However, in many countries, wood is plentiful, and several kinds of animals are well adapted to eating it. They are able to turn wood into nutritious meals.

Some of these animals feed on wood even *after* people have made it into furniture and other items. In a previous chapter, you read about porcupines that crunch up wooden tools, walls, and oars. Even big animals, such as elephants, sometimes eat burned house lumber and ash to get sodium.

Larvae of insects called timber borers tunnel through wood for two to three years, feeding as they go. Their menu includes telephone poles, fence posts, and ties used on train tracks.

But the greatest number of wood feeders are insects, and for most of them, wood is a "boring" thing. Old-house borers even got their name from their habit of boring through wood in old houses and other buildings in Europe. In North America, these insects feed on new buildings, too. All old-house borers seem to prefer pine and spruce wood.

The adults lay rows of eggs in splits or cracks in wood, where the larvae feed for up to five years. They're noisy eaters. You can hear them "tick, tick, tick" as they scrape the wood. Then they make holes at the surface when they leave to live their short adult lives of up to 16 days.

Also ticking through the timbers are deathwatch beetles. But they tick as adults, not as larvae. The females beat their heads against their burrows to call for mates. The noise has triggered many stories

A shiny beauty, this flatheaded wood borer lays its eggs in a tree. When the larvae hatch, they eat the wood, even after it is made into boards or furniture.

The larvae of flatheaded or metallic wood borers sometimes live in dry wood inside houses. They take more than 25 years to mature, all the while chomping up wood with their spoon-shaped, toothy mouthparts.

of haunted houses. It has also led to the belief that deathwatch beetles are a sign of death, which is how they got their name.

These beetles lay their eggs in wood, then the larvae mine it. Their home—and banquet—of wood may be turned into walls, desks, tables, and chairs while they are still inside it. People may not know the beetles are there until a chair or table falls apart or a floor caves in.

The most well-known wood eater is the termite, an insect many people call the white ant. Termites are not related to ants but they look a bit like them, and they form large colonies like ants do. Many live in warm, tropical countries, but some live in cooler places, such as Canada and the United States.

Although they eat some dead insects for protein, most kinds of termites feed almost entirely on wood. Inside the termites live protozoans, tiny one-celled life forms that break wood down into bits of sugar that the insects can digest. In return, the protozoans get safe and cozy mobile homes.

Termites may live in small colonies of about 50 or huge colonies of several million. Each one has a king and queen, whose job it is to produce more termites. Others in the colony do all the work, cleaning up, feeding, and looking after the royal couple and their young. Some colonies have workers that act as soldiers to defend their relatives from danger.

Termites feed on almost anything made of wood, including buildings and furniture of all kinds. They gnaw the wood, then feed others in their colony—from mouth to mouth or from back end to mouth. During the feedings, they pass some of the protozoans to the young so they can digest their food.

Termites that eat wood can reduce a table to a pile of sawdust. Their queen is a giant egg-laying machine that exists to produce more and more termites.

Not all wood eaters lodge on land. Seagoing creatures called gribbles, or pinworms, turn up in wooden boats, floats, piers, and pilings around the world. They eat so much wood that some people call them "termites of the sea." But they're not insects; they're related to lobsters and crabs.

One common kind of gribble is only .12 inch (.3 centimetre) long. But it can scrape its way through wood quite fast. It usually tunnels close to the surface of the wood. If the roof starts to cave in or peel away, the gribble makes a new tunnel. Wood gives gribbles most of the nutrients they need. They may also eat a bit of fungus for extra nitrogen.

The size of a gang of gribbles grows constantly. As soon as new gribbles hatch, they join the other nibblers. And there goes more wood.

Paper Is Perfect!

In 1187, the first black rats found in the British Isles upset a bishop by gnawing his books. He is believed to have put a curse on the rats to get rid of them. It didn't work. Rats and their smaller cousins, mice, still gnaw books in the British Isles and many other places in the world. Although they eat a wide range of food, they sometimes snack on paper and glue.

Another occasional paper eater is the great black slug. It is great in size—about 6 inches (15 centimetres) long—but it's not always black. In fact, the great black slug comes in several colors.

Most of the time, this slug eats plants, but it may feed on other things when they're handy. At a publishing office in London, England, some great black slugs fed on coloring material used in book covers.

Model Mound

While some kinds of termites destroy buildings, other kinds show people how to make buildings better. In the African country of Zimbabwe, a new office tower owes its design to a termite colony.

This colony of a million termites feeds on fungus that it grows inside a mound of dung and mud up to 30 feet (9 metres) tall. The fungus needs a steady temperature to grow. The mound's design helps control the breezes coming in from outside, cooling or warming the mound.

Using the termite mound as a model for the Zimbabwe office tower, architects created a building that is saving millions of dollars. It uses less than 10 percent of the energy other buildings use to cool or warm the inside air.

Devouring parts of a good book is an easy matter for a great black slug with a toothy tongue.

One slug that was kept indoors for two days started to eat a newspaper, a copy of *The New York Times*. It worked its way through the news very easily. Slugs scrape food using a rough tongue covered with hundreds—sometimes thousands—of sharp teeth. The tongue never loses its scraping power. As its teeth wear out, new ones move in to replace them.

A silvery, fish-shaped insect called a silverfish thrives on paper in homes in many parts of the world. Although it can't fly, the silverfish moves around on quick feet to feed. Mostly it gobbles up tiny bits of wallpaper, cellophane, and books, including everything that books are made of. It goes after protein in the bookbinding glues and the pastelike material on book covers, as well as starch in the paper.

Jawlike mouthparts grind the food up first, then teeth in an inner pouch grind it further. Silverfish can digest even the toughest paper easily. They feed at night, using long antennae to guide them. But you might guess they have been at your books if you notice pages with holes and chewed edges. You might even spot some telltale silver through a magnifying glass. The scales of silverfish rub off easily.

Another super survivor is the cockroach. One of the oldest insects on Earth, it has been around for about 300 million years. Some kinds live indoors with people. The German cockroach, for instance, lives in human homes worldwide. It settles almost any place that offers warmth, food, moisture, and places to hide. It also shows up in stores, warehouses, factories, office buildings, and ships.

The flat, brown body of the German cockroach—about .6 inch (1.5 centimetres) long—slips easily under doors and through cracks only .06 inch (.15 centimetre) wide. Like the silverfish, it finds food mostly at night by using its two long antennae as guides. Sensors in the roach's knees warn it of moving objects, animals, or people nearby. It can even detect the footsteps of another cockroach.

Smell and touch lead this insect to dinner, which could be paper products, such as books, stamps, or wallpaper, and just about anything else: house insulation, wood, clothing, ink, or shoe polish. Sometimes a cockroach munches on electric cords from televisions and computers, even causing fires now and then. And if there are so many cockroaches that food is scarce, they may gnaw toenails and thick skin on people's feet.

Pale, wingless insects called booklice eat the paper and paste in books. You probably can't see them, but you may be able to hear them tap, tap, tap against the books with a knob near their tail.

COCKROACH CRAZES

When sailors are at sea, they have fewer games to play. So for centuries, they held cockroach races on many of their voyages. The insects were easy to find on any ship, and they were great to race. Cockroaches run very fast.

On land, people found other uses for them. Some kept cockroaches—especially the big Madagascar roaches—as pets. They grow up to 3 inches (7.5 centimetres) long. And they clean and groom themselves as well as cats do.

Parents sometimes gave medicine made of cockroaches to their children to get rid of worms and to treat some illnesses, such as epilepsy.

In France and Russia, many people believed that good luck followed cockroaches into a house. They thought the insects protected them. People in Ireland and the southern United States, however, assumed that roaches brought bad luck. They believed the insects were really witches and blamed them for bad crops.

Out of fear, people tried to get rid of cockroaches. But they used some strange methods: waiting for Good Friday to sweep the insects out, putting jars in the fireplace overnight to trap them, and sticking a pin in one roach to scare away the others. Of all their efforts, the most successful was taking the cockroaches to a neighbor's house—but that didn't win any friends.

Using thousands of tiny hairs on feelerlike mouthparts, the cockroach tastes its food before it feeds. That sometimes saves its life, helping it avoid poison that people may set out to kill it. After the wood-eating cockroach dines, protozoans that live inside it help to break down the food.

Material Is Marvelous!

People everywhere use all sorts of material to make things they want for themselves and their homes: blankets, curtains, carpets, clothing, and more. But to some animals, these things are just more yummy food. The most popular products are made of materials that came from animals in the first place, such as wool, fur, mohair (from goats), silk (from silkworms), and leather.

The animals that eat most human goods are the beetles and moths that can digest this tougher food. Unlike most animals, they easily break down materials such as wool and fur to get protein.

Small, oval-shaped carpet beetles often lay their eggs on wool carpets. That gives their bristly larvae food to eat the minute they hatch. The larvae also eat up any hair and lint that may gather in corners or cracks in houses. The black carpet beetle is one of the biggest carpet feeders in the world. Although the female—who lives just two to four weeks as an adult—eats only pollen, she may leave 100 hungry larvae in a house. They can spend up to three years chomping through somebody's carpet or upholstered couch.

The hairy larvae of larder beetles attack materials in teddy bears, wool sweaters, and food-stained clothes around the world. Some are called hide beetles because they prefer chewing items made from animal hides. Thousands of years ago, they moved into ancient tombs to feed on Egyptian mummies. Today, some museums use them to clean off animal bones for studies and displays. The beetles gnaw steadily, feeding in and around all the crannies of a skeleton. A team of 60 beetles can completely clean a bird's bones in three days.

Tucked safely inside their cases, clothes moth larvae live up to four years. These ones are munching a nutritious woolen scarf.

MOTHS AWAY

If you don't want moths eating your clothes, you can try these methods to keep them away.

- Take carpets out of dark closets where moths might breed.
- Clean and air clothes before storing them.
- Hang containers of mothballs—strong smelling crystals—in closets and storage bags.

And just for fun, here are a couple of old ideas (definitely *not* guaranteed to work).

- Swoop up adult moths—two at a time—using a long net with a short net inside. The man who made this tool in the 1880s claimed that air would force the first insect through the short net into the long net. That left the short net free to catch the second insect.
- Hunt moths with a gun invented in 1905. Fire the trigger and a steel rod zooms out. Two metal flaps at the end of the rod snap together. If you're VERY lucky, you'll squish a moth between them.

On satiny wings, little clothes moths fly weakly from house to house almost everywhere. They lay eggs in dark, quiet places, such as storage closets. About five days later, their larvae hatch and start feeding on wool, silk, and fur clothing that is seldom moved. In fact, they can't survive on clothes that people wear often.

The larvae get protein from the clothing and from any hair they find on it. And by nibbling stains from food, sweat, and saliva, they get some of their vitamins.

Some kinds of clothes moth larvae make thin, portable cases to protect themselves. Each case is made of silk plus bits of the clothes the larvae eat. Shaped like tubes, the tiny cases are open at each end, and the larvae feed safely inside.

There's no denying it. Animals do a lot of damage to homes and many of the things people make. That damage costs some countries millions of dollars every year. Still, the keen appetites of many of these animals play an important role in reducing garbage and unwanted products.

Tears, toenails, dandruff, and dung. Animals really DO eat the weirdest things—things that people aren't eager to find on their own dinner plates. But this odd food makes nutritious, easy-to-find meals for a great many animals. And that's a very good thing. If all animals were as picky about their food as we are, they'd have a much tougher time surviving, and we'd have a huge mess to clean up. Here's to all the hearty appetites around us!

HOME-STYLE MEALS

- Some kinds of cockroaches have always lived with people, even when a human home was no more than a cave.
- Wood-chomping termites can get the bite on books as well as walls, stairs, and posts.
- Silverfish eat starch wherever they find it, even in stiffly starched collars and cuffs.
- Cool fall weather brings crickets into houses. Not only do they chirp a lot, they chew woolen clothes and carpets.

INDEX

ACKNOWLEDGMENTS

Fascinated by a magazine article on dung-eating beetles, Colleen MacMillan phoned to ask: "What other strange foods do animals eat?" And the idea for this book was born. I am greatly indebted to Colleen, not only for sparking a venture that led me through more than a year of particularly engrossing research, but for enthusiastically supporting and encouraging my efforts ever since I began to write nature books. Thanks, Colleen, for being a mentor and a friend.

After I had drafted a manuscript that included hundreds of animals from tiny insects to large mammals, literally from around the globe, I set out to locate a scientist who could and would take on the daunting task of reviewing it for accuracy. Dr. Lawrence Dill of Simon Fraser University in Burnaby, British Columbia, more than filled the bill. His eager and conscientious efforts are deeply appreciated. During his review, he consulted about a dozen members of the Behavioural Ecology Research Group, which he directs. My gratitude extends to them as well.

That brings me to a very special acknowledgment to scientists everywhere. While researching my books, I am always in awe of the tremendous efforts scientists make to unravel the many mysteries of this world. There are those who spend hours a day peering up hollow trees to record the social behavior of bats; those who travel the Amazon to study giant tarantulas; and those who painstakingly probe the natural world in laboratories. To them, a very sincere note of thanks for helping us all become better acquainted with the planet we share.

To Terry Smith, artist superb, goes my gratitude for producing the stunning paintings that grace this book. Besides her extraordinary skills as a wildlife painter, I want to acknowledge the meticulous efforts she makes in researching each of the subjects in her paintings and in making them come alive with her striking use of color.

Three young people, Elly Knight, Taylor McLean, and Nathan McLean, who read the first draft of this book, offered insightful comments that were wonderfully helpful. Eager writers, after all, do not exist without eager readers.

And as always, I more than appreciate the patience and cheerful support of Wayne, my lifetime friend and partner.